The Thin Veneer

Fourteen Lines of Fracture

Clifford Lile

GW00578692

The Thin Veneer

© Clifford Liles

First Edition 2022

Clifford Liles has asserted his authorship and given permission to Dempsey & Windle
for these poems to be published here.

Published by Dempsey & Windle

15 Rosetrees
Guildford
Surrey
GU1 2HS
UK
01483 571164
dempseyandwindle.com

A catalogue record for this book is available from the British Library

British Library Cataloguing-in-Publication Data

ISBN: 978-1-913329-81-5

Printed and bound in the UK

To my wife, Gillian.

Clifford Liles was born in Kent but now lives in Herefordshire. He has travelled, lived and worked in several countries throughout Europe and in Australia, during which he experienced several numinous moments – for which there were rarely photographs. In more settled times, wanting to recall, to create, he discovered the sonnet: that indivisible expression of a moment.

The Thin Veneer explores themes such as the fragility of our existence and relationships, the power of nature, the impact of technology and the climate breakdown.

Open this collection of sonnets and open a window onto all that stands between civilisation and its loss: the thin veneer. In each fourteen lines of fracture, you will read of loss, jealousy and betrayal; of solitude and those moments between life and death.

Contents

Life

At the Tumbleweed Diner

DAYBREAK

From the furthest booth,
you can gaze out at dust devils.
By the window there, you sit on the shore of a burning day.
A Corvette slumbers in the dawn light, caught in fish bones of the car lot. Beyond,
the unbound scrubland. You feel the bitter hug of your first coffee.
Bottomless. Catch the glint of a jetliner's trail,
silver sum of a hundred lives departing.
You hail a waitress as she glides by.

SUNDOWN

Over the car lot, figments of lanterns hang,
hanging in the glassed-off mirk. You savour the mood. A burgeoning quiet.
In this moth-light, you tip your mug. Deepen the dregs. A bystander to the blacktop.
The Corvette's gone. Faces forgotten.
Ketchup stains and coffee rings remain.
A waitress wheels out a pail and mop.

Requiem for a Kayaker

Dies Irae

Behold, this loud altar, a cataract
all draped in thunder; this throng of hushed ferns
and rushes. In the shallows, a kayak.
Did strength leave him? What left his boat upturned?

Offertorio

This man, who but for neoprene is naked,
drifts by beeches hewn from time as soaring pillars.
A nave of Nature, still as roots and mud,
where man's survival turns on strength and skill.

Libera Me

Past timeless trees, flowing ever downwards;
his paddle's gone, surrendered to the rapids.
Torrents crash. This surge slicks darkly seawards.
It passes empty scrubland, wild and arid.

Lux Aeterna

A clearing opens in the wilderness;
a bright salvation, where he comes to rest.

Looking West across Snake River to Grand Teton Mountain
In Memoriam Ansel Adams

No witness but me to this wreck of heaven,
fallen-in, a cloud-crash of blue-marbled ice.
Fixing this scene, I scan titanic spires.
Down those sheer crags, a man would drop for ten

seconds. A mote of screaming life. I watch
eagles soar, ten minutes, thermalling up.
I clatter out my tripod, set the shutter,
the lens to wide-angle, wipe off a smudge.

Waiting. Clouds, my seconds; scudding showers,
my minutes. Wool shirt sticking on cold sweat.
My sky will be perfect black; ice fields, white.
This, my last ascent. No want of reminders –

the struggling for breath. Then, in the viewer,
perfection! This study of solitude.

A Checkpoint Missed Near the Guatemalan Border

Poetic a passport is not: DOB,
Birthplace. He fillets the car seats (gaunt hands;
nicotine at fifteen?) My pack lands brand up.
He flicks through my past travels, in jungle heat.
La, la, la, just look down. Stood on wild loam
miles from the modern. La, la, ... tarantula.
He orders his soldiers to strip my Toyota.
(I'd driven hard, eyes on the road alone.
Rifles had hovered like iron dragonflies.
I'd overshot ... braked ... a comet of dust.)
He fastens his buttons. An air of corruption,
or burnt brakes? And with those gunmetal eyes
he stares at me. Slips into his pocket
the blood-red passport of a live poet.

Snowbound

Starving! My last hot meal was just warm porridge.
I climb, with crunching boots through pristine snow,
and pass the refuge, following yellow poles.
A headache of haste before the pass closes.

My tunnel of garb flaps as the wind strengthens.
It comes galumphing down from icebound peaks
then vents as if there was a tear in heaven,
buffeting my cupped match of body heat.

Across these crumpled rags of hills that spread
all the way to winter, threadbare and old,
I struggle on, with a less certain tread.
Under an acetylene sun, yet cold,
      I stagger. Kick icy feathers like a clown,
      then lay my head and soul on weightless down.

No Work Today

While freezing clouds come teeming down in crumbs,
he sprawls, unspooled, at the end of night's tether.
On ground that's anvil-cold, his limbs are numb.
Roused, hungry, again he breakfasts on foetid air.

There is no break of day; it grows like a stain.
Rucksacks crawl through the phosphorescent gloom,
this place where bottom-dwelling creatures reign.
And where his breath has frozen, crystal posies bloom.

He unzips the tent, hears the blizzard's hiss,
sees the cold swell engulfing his cocoon.
From jumbled thoughts, one surges to the surface:
It shouts: *You should dig yourself out and soon.*
      Don't forget! So long since he last slept
      that shreds of sleep like snowflakes fall. And he forgets.

Murdering Gully

Instructions: Pitch the tent where not too steep.
I climbed this ravine, left the wilderness,
quit the green tangle of Kanangra Deep.
Pitch tent where undergrowth is clearest.

By monumental cliffs, a slum of ferns;
I hacked and grubbed a grave-sized patch of ground.
I'd trekked beyond the point of no return,
lost, as dusk fell. Would I ever be found?

Pitch in a dry place. Then came the downpour,
an alien rain that curdled the soil.
Use pegs to anchor to the forest floor.
I stopped the tent's downward slide with a coil
of rope, squirmed inside the chrysalis sack.
Leeches crawled up my face in the pitch black.

Washing Machines

A cog, a lever, an iron gyre of suds,
a countdown to zero on a display pane;
interlocked, this cycle ends with a thud.

We don't know the programme so let's begin.
What washes infant clothes without complaint?
A cog, a lever, an iron gyre of suds.

Schools over; end of term and discipline.
A fallen branch, a bike ride in the rain:
interlocked, this cycle ends with a thud.

A shirt for work - sweat, coffee and aspirin.
What machine could remove these stains?
A cog, a lever, an iron gyre of suds.

Round and round the scene of jazz clubs and gin.
Bass riffs and drum breaks sound over again,
interlocked, this cycle ends with a thud.

There's so much gone by, we're all in a spin.
It's time to wash bibs and nappies again.
A cog, a lever, an iron gyre of suds,
interlocked, this whole cycle ends with a thud.

Relationships

Watching the Moon Landing

Dad roused me and whispered: *shush, it's still night!*
I yomped down knee-high stairs in the darkness,
landed on plush carpet: mother's purchase.
Upstairs, her door was shut, glossy and white.

Dad buttered squares of toast by the fridge light.
Shopping lists lay latent on a bleached surface,
set out like nonsense poems. We left the airless
room. He ignored the crumbs, to my delight.

We watched a flag, planted by a spectre,
blowing in no breeze on 'Live News' on TV;
the screen's glimmering black and white exposed
the settee, grey as moon rock ejecta.
In that vacuum, Dad made one giant leap.
His marriage was a gloss. A door now closed.

Do Men Consider Consequences?

Second floor, she says. She buzzes me in.
We chat amongst the desiccated stacks
covering Kant, Descartes and coffee tables –
neither of us mentioning him.

I've brought a bottle of wine, red wine,
so we move, laughing, into his kitchen.
She's a turbulence of smiles and just-washed hair.
I pinball around for glasses and thoughts.
Pointing, she tip-toes, cashmere riding up.
I reach. She follows my raised arm, braiding it,
proffering herself against my body.

My resolve falters in a fog of Grenache:
she is his; she is not mine. But, in rut,
I forget. Forget all the consequences
when she touches ….

A Seamstress Considers Her Options

The trap awaits outside. Its horse, a bay,
jangling its traces by dank stone walls.
With her income gone, life has spun away
like moon-bright shillings dropped down a well.

Before a mirror and peonies, red
as her nightmares, she begins her theatre
of poisons: gathers her powdered white lead;
and black moon-shaped patches of taffeta.

She mouths a humid oath then covers her scars;
touches rouge to her lips, feeling the pink sting.
There. Ready, she thinks (but her shaking marks
the proximity of panic and skin),
   for the lamp-lit stage; the candle-lit trysts.
   For the age-old trap that men can't resist.

Jealousy

Once bingo, now a ballroom, the Folkestone Leas:
on stage, the judges sat like four front teeth.

Now only the best of the couples remained.
My wife, you were cool as a waltz in the heats,
crossing parquet all polish and silvery rain,
like the sweep of a taffeta sunbeam.

I stood out, with two left feet and no tuxedo;
between each dance, I polished up your heels.

In the Latin the shadowy faces, beguiled
by your bonfire of passions, your partner's vain tango,
by the sequined audacity, fake tan and smiles,
didn't see him seduce with his hips to and fro.

       At each climactic lift, his hand would linger
       behind your back, all gypsy rings and fingers.

A Bitter Breakfast

All I heard in sullen double basses
and shrill horns was betrayal in music.
Those chords that echoed through our living space
chilled our flat, our lounge, our single bedroom.

A letter addressed to us; meant for you.

A bitter breakfast. Then the quiet tide
of morning light began to freeze around
those words. Long held. Barbed wire on ice and white.
The reading of them. My shock of seeing:

a crystal skein – a foetal ultrasound.

So before the end of that adagio,
before all was frozen, I understood
why you, on Saturday, a month ago,
packed, pulled off your ring and left me for good.

Enduring Solitude

Not one word had passed my lips since dawn broke.
I roamed that winter park of beasts alone,
past empty pens, while through a stand of pines
swept a whispering wind, sharp as broken bone.

Between the stark, sleet-wet columns, I glimpsed
bison, like some far archipelago,
their moist eyes dully leaking out their lives.
The herd not heeding if I stay or go.

At dusk, I sat inside a vaulted café
of leather, candles, linen and champagne,
and other singles, caught in mirrors, mused
their fate. Should I go, or, perhaps remain?
   Not a word, not one utterance since dawn,
   then a waitress asked me: *why so forlorn?*

Society

Storms Across Europe

Blowing hot, all high pressure since last week,
but snowstorms then surged past the calm Azores,
blowing cold. All signs show the outlook's bleak.

El Pais flutters with news of yesterday;
skull-like villas gaze out on silent shores.
Blowing hot, all high pressure since last week.

A steel-hued sea freights in a nor-westerly,
it skirts the crowded Shamrock rattling doors,
blowing cold. All signs show the outlook's bleak.

The waiters idle, all strop and lethargy,
near the Parthenon, in the new agoras.
Blowing hot, all high pressure since last week.

Yells from Bingo halls distract the elderly
from storms that scour this town of discount stores,
blowing cold. All signs show the outlook's bleak.

Politicians talk, briefed so expertly
(they'll finish soon the BBC assures):
blowing hot, all high pressure since last week;
blowing cold, all signs show the outlook's bleak.

Doodlebug

A carriage clock. It ticks above the fire.
Smells of coal tar soap mixed with chimney smoke.
A kettle exhales. Hob hot on gas jets,
clouding up the garden view where raindrops
burst in marcasite pools. But not one sound
disturbs the placid room. Photos arranged
on shelves. A lamp lit to fend off nightfall.

Here stands a wireless, a model Spitfire,
threadbare armchairs that reek of cigar smoke.
High tea is set. A vase as black as jet
with long stemmed roses. Faded. A petal drops.
Far overhead a droning engine's sound.
Insignificant. Muffled by the rain.
It sputters out, then silence falls.

Footnote: The V1 self-propelled bomb, nicknamed the Doodlebug, terrorised London
during the Second World War. It was launched from across the Channel and would
fly unpiloted until it ran out of fuel. Then the engine would cut out leaving the one-
ton bomb to fall on the houses below.

The Density of Loss

In Munich, the Munich of comforts, stands
this bridge: a barrage over river flats, plaited and drab,
where winter invites itself in.

I watch a stranger pass below. Naked,
yet draped in an ochre blanket crusted in ice.
Chanting nonsense, his sandals plosh on gravel banks.

In the weeping cold, a swan broods, reflecting itself.
Head bowed against the hiss of sleet, the density of loss.
I grip the parapet of this concrete span.
Behind me, pass the trams.

Packed full. Pale faces condensing on the panes.
Do they watch me? A scarecrow in a scarf.
Or him? Our prospects thin as splintered ice.
My heart is stained with shadows. We are jetsam.

Running Fifth Avenue

On this island, off the coast of itself,
in high acres of glass the clouds are trapped,
while shivelight gleams through the silos of cash.

He stares. Standing on the sidewalk. A deep well
of vertigo. A matted blanket wrapped
around his shoulders. No scraps in the trash.

Poised, with violent eyes like a black bear.
People pass. In that old light of slow blues,
all of their shoes teem past like river salmon.

Envy possesses him, creeps from its lair.
He spies a girl's purse, the leather strap loose;
she's silver sunlight on the stream of Mammon.
       For her that ardent morning had begun –
       so well. He fixes his prey. Then he runs.

Seen Through a Prism of People

A busy road quarrels with the fractious heat,
snaps back at a tap of snares, throb of a song,
as waves of protesters pulse through this street.
Buoyant chests and flashing teeth of all ages;

a rapture of young lungs knowing they're not wrong.

Banners unfurl like eels, flyers like lures.
We see others in their littering wake: touts
hawking T-shirts, and partially obscured,
heavier men with bottles itching to fly.

From their angry placards they have no doubts.

The grammar of their grievance stops debate.
But mannequins observe with shop-soiled eyes,
while CCTVs glare with glass and hate:
imprinting one truth of the many lies.

Coup d'Etat

Beads of wine dot this long and polished bar.
High above town: men talk, their voices low.
Strains of jazz. Reefs of crystal glasses glow.
Waiters bask, slip through pools of light like sharks.

Few drinkers left. One minute to midnight.
The reflection of my wine, an echo
of mine, suggests an hourglass. Time slows.
Outside, the city's embers re-ignite.

Towards the east is another reflection:
of four men in the panes, shadows of greed.
Three charcoal suits; one pale. Conspirators.
The fourth rants and shouts of insurrection.
I raise my glass as if to kiss. It bleeds.
Outside, buildings burn, torched by rioters.

The Isle of the Dead
After Arnold Boecklin's painting

This gleaming shroud, these waters haunted and grave.
A creak of wood, dull thud and slosh of oars,
their bubbling wake: these were the only sounds.
I scanned the sky – not even a bird calling.
A skin of winter steel as flat as glass,
and mats of algae, rust red, stained this sea.

I asked the man for one last chance to see
what was once home. Its brooding contours, graven
in stone, reflected in the oily glass.
This lone boat shuddered as he pulled one oar;
hove to, the isle in sight, when *halt* I called.
I rose to look. He fussed with weights and soundings.

A chance to remember those smells and sounds:
deep tolling from the belfry by the sea;
sweet blooms of yeast from bakers. I recalled:
the clock with roman numerals engraved
and cries of children when it chimed the hours;
the wash of sibilant prayers on stained glass.

Now red shards, piles of broken glass;
fragments of that past. Nothing stirred. No sound.
The cypress trees were still. I stood in awe
at blasted ramparts foundered in the sea,
like raw seams of coal. We were heedless how grave
our peril, what demon names we were called.

They'd come so suddenly. To make the call
was difficult. No time to raise a glass
with friends, debate our plight. No time to grieve.
Our flat lives folded when those shots resounded,
those angry coughs of dogs. We felt at sea,
unsure of our horizon. Cannons roared.

Our homes shook. We'd fled. As if for war or
invasion by some race of fearsome calling,
we ran toward the deep and gleaming sea.
Spray. Streets of bloody spray. Spumes of glass
exploded. And more, until no screams resounded.
Then we were rolled in shrouds and into graves.

I faced the oarsman, met his eyes of glass:
what are you called? He pointed without sound
to his seat where *Charon* was engraved.

Civilisation

The Fall of Rome

A wheeled refuse bin wobbles as a fly
takes off, crashes into the café's window,
cracks it. Over-priced sponges sweat, muffins
topple as if by a quake. Nothing sold yet
from wire columns tiled with cards and leaflets
of Roman mosaics. It's end of season
for the displays of weekend legionnaires.
Crumbs dot uncleared plastic tables; spittle
from crowds the day before. Their food smells linger.

The fat and sallow-faced manager drags
a refuse sack outside, then waddles back,
fails to close the door. The fly careens in,
vandalising tables, chairs – comes to rest,
wings smearing ketchup. A mosaic of mess.

Ship of Fools

Faint petals of my dream detached and fell,
disturbed by an oncoming man-made thrumming,
vibrating air where countless moths were swarming
in the glow of lamps, bright as night dispelled.

There came a strange machine, by steam propelled.
Huge as a siege-tower, such momentum,
crawled along with hidden pistons drumming,
as if by living herds of wheels impelled.

A party jazzed upon its upper decks:
a crowd that jived; a lantern-lit parade.
Who is at the controls? I asked. They gasped.
Silence. Their faces, late-night white, perplexed,
as if auroral thoughts had caught and faded,
then their chit-chat, their gibber rumbled past.

The Promise of Magic

All eyes are on the high-wire act, none
on the wires, as she twist-twirls to screams
of delight. Below, the crowds are gorging on fun
and candyfloss in a darkness lanced by beams
of spotlights. Trailing cables coil, humming
like wasps in the wings where scaffolds of magic gleam.
Where foremen count out coins for clowns and tumblers.

*

On a horizon left ajar for dawn, cumulus promise
floods. As he walks his dog across the Downs,
barking breaks the morning's newly minted stillness.
Halfway to briar seams, his Border Collie has found
not his stick of dog-spit and dew but some menace;
faces of clowns on flyers, flattened ground,
the grass as dead as the big top's promise.

Highway of Hail

So calm in my car. The traffic's fat with speed,
drowsy shadows from flyovers flit by
as dark cumulus glide over windscreens.

I let them overtake, these faceless drivers
facing forward into days far from placid.
Sunglasses click shut to a green-hued sky.

The first strike cracks my windscreen. I shrink back
from the hyper-kinetic spider striking
this thin veneer. Some cars swerve, some zigzag.

Then, white clatter widows the world outside,
louder and louder like rocks hurled at metal.
A burst of glass shards lands between my thighs.

Foot down, I race to a flyover's shelter,
cutting up others in this helter-skelter.

Litter Pick

Dressed in Hi-Vis, we wade on. Black sacks bunched.
Our glass percussion of jars and jangling tins.
Through stubbled fields, the river witters past. It clutches
our calves. Tells us lurid tales of burst banks and ruins.
We poke the nettles with pickers for plastic, hung out as prayer flags;
shattered bottles lie like jewels scattered from rotted coffins.

We banter about our score, our tally of bags.
With a pulley, heave out shopping trolleys buried in ferns.
The undertow, like some rising tsunami under silken shrouds, drags
us downstream. A surge foams around a rusted bike. The river turns
around a bend, a tipping point, reveals to us all its works. We arrive
at a stone bridge, collapsed; a pile-up of cars, some over-turned.

Our mood dies in a funeral of smiles. No sighs of survivors.
Our discarded sacks float on like black swans. I telephone an SOS.
In the wreckage, a Hyundai and its driver,
      not driving – her grey tresses
      billowing – dead as her dress.

Terra Incognita

This is God's own country, he says to his son
through fierce tears. But the terracotta dirt
is dry as clinker. A leafless ghost gum
fingernails the sky as insectile heat
enfolds him, intimate as death, feasting
on sweat. Out of sight, in his scungy kitchen,
his tap drips. Once. From out of the hot nowhere
a zephyr swirls. A flyscreen door bangs.

His rows of wheat lie flat like torn up shrouds.
Each full dark the empty dingoes stray in,
tongues lolling. Their tattoo of want a necklace
round his house. He whispers to his son: *Never
seen the like of this.* But his son is out,
a truckie hauling water to the towns.

The Arrow of Time

Quiet. I squint across the chainmail sea through
a blood-starred windscreen. In chaos and shit.
Seawater chills my lap. A reek of sewage.
Shadows of debris tattoo my pale arms.

My lone cry keens to a vast simplicity.

*

Blackout. Then, from my mind, the darkness drains.
Images surface: of billboards, freeways,
of cars like blisters burst, dust and bloodstains,
of cracks and walls. These: twisted, fallen, charred.

This brutal minute, I see towers sway.

*

8am. My car's interior mutes
the evil traffic's jazz. Deep sea squid lying
on the beach: soft and dead; while bored commuters
drive past. Why, why am I so unquiet?

Thanks and Acknowledgements

I would like to thank the following people for their invaluable advice or help:

Dr Angela France, Senior Lecturer in Creative Writing, University of Gloucestershire;

Dr Sonia Overall, MA Creative Writing Lead, Senior Lecturer, Canterbury Christ Church University;

Professor Jan Pahl CBE, D.Litt.;

Peter Erftemeijer, Mot Juste, www.motjuste.co.uk;

Cover Image post-production: Sanjay Kalideen.

And my wife for her constant support from the beginning.

*

Thanks are also due to the editors and judges of the books, journals, e-zines and competitions where some of these poems have appeared before.

Previously published poems

Dream Catcher	'Terra Incognita'	2022
Graffiti	'Jealousy'	2021
Reach Poetry:	'Washing Machines'	2021
	'A Checkpoint Missed Near the Guatemalan Border'	2019
	Coup d'Etat	2019

Orbis	'The Promise of Magic'	2020
	'At the Tumbleweed Diner'	2020
London Grip	'A Seamstress Considers Her Options'	2020
The Cannon's Mouth	'The Arrow of Time'	2019
	'Doodlebug'	2018

Competitions

'Requiem for a Kayaker'	Early Works Press Competition, August 2020: Runner-up. Canterbury Festival Poet of the Year Competition 2014: Longlisted.
'The Isle of the Dead'	Sandwich Arts Week Poetry Competition 2018: 2nd Place.
'Jealousy'	Sandwich Arts Week Poetry Competition 2018: shortlisted
'Doodlebug'	University of Winchester Writers' Festival Competition 2017: Highly Commended.
'Enduring Solitude'	Writers' Forum Competition, August 2014: runner-up.
'Murdering Gully', 'Storms Across Europe', and 'Ship of Fools'	Canterbury Festival Poet of the Year Competition 2013: all shortlisted.